How Grapes Become Raisins

by Kris Bonnell

Here are some grape vines.
Grapes come from grape vines.
Raisins come from grapes.

3

4

The grapes on the vines are green.
Most raisins come from green grapes.

The grapes are picked off the vines and put into the sun.

They will dry in the sun.

7

The grapes are drying in the sun.
The grapes are not green anymore.
They are black.
The grapes are not grapes anymore.

9

The grapes are raisins!

The raisins are put into boxes for us to eat.